DEVOPS LEADERSHIP - STEPS FOR THE INTRODUCTION AND IMPLEMENTATION OF DEVOPS

SUCCESSFUL TRANSFORMATION FROM SILO TO VALUE CHAIN

MARTIN J. ADAMS

Copyright © Martin J. Adams
All Rights Reserved.

ISBN 978-1-63904-107-7

This book has been published with all efforts taken to make the material error-free after the consent of the author. However, the author and the publisher do not assume and hereby disclaim any liability to any party for any loss, damage, or disruption caused by errors or omissions, whether such errors or omissions result from negligence, accident, or any other cause.

While every effort has been made to avoid any mistake or omission, this publication is being sold on the condition and understanding that neither the author nor the publishers or printers would be liable in any manner to any person by reason of any mistake or omission in this publication or for any action taken or omitted to be taken or advice rendered or accepted on the basis of this work. For any defect in printing or binding the publishers will be liable only to replace the defective copy by another copy of this work then available.

Contents

Preface	v
1. What Does Devops Mean?	1
2. Continuous ...	11
3. What Is Devops Leadership?	13
4. Change According To Lewin And The Continuous Improvement	17
5. Steps For The Introduction And Optimization Of Devops	20
Afterword	55
Literature List	57

Preface

"DevOps means agile IT (operations) delivery, which is what is required to match the rhythm of agile IT development. DevOps is a philosophy, not a method, a model, a body of knowledge, or *shudder* a purchasable tool. DevOps is the philosophy of unifying development and operations at the culture, practice, and tool levels to achieve faster and more frequent implementation of changes in production.

- *Culture=behavior, collaboration, accountability/liability, trust/empowerment....*
- *Practice=principle, roles/RACI, processes/procedures, metrics/reporting, KPIs/improvement....*
- *Tooling=Shared knowledge, mutual tooling, common technology platforms_...* [1] "

When we talk about DevOps, it's not that simple. Depending on who you talk to, DevOps means something completely different. It seems to be somehow related to the other meanings and interpretations, but it is nevertheless so far removed from other views in everyday life that exponents of different approaches and approaches have a hard time finding a common basis for conversation.

In this book, we will look at the topic of DevOps from a leadership perspective. This means that we will look in particular at the aspects relating to culture and model and, of course, gain an overview of the various methods used. In addition, we will deal with heavyweight topics such as leadership in the DevOps context as well as the important question of the introduction and development of DevOps from a leadership perspective in this context, and from this we will work out requirements for the role and task of leadership in the agile context, particularly in the context of DevOps.

PREFACE

[1] Rob England: Define DevOps. What is DevOps? In: The IT Skeptic. November 29, 2014, accessed February 17, 2016 (English).

ONE
WHAT DOES DEVOPS MEAN?

DevOps focuses on a collaboration between development and operations that emphasizes a change in mindset, better collaboration and tighter integration. It does this by combining a wide variety of concepts and techniques to be more efficient, innovate faster, and deliver more value to businesses and customers.

The history of DevOps

The beginning of the DevOps movement can be traced back to the first decade of the 21st century. It emerged as a reaction to the identified conflicting goals of two areas in corporate IT.

On the one hand, there was the development area, whose task is to develop new solutions to problems as quickly as possible and put them into operation. On the other hand, there was IT operations, whose task was to ensure the stability, security and continuity of the existing solution in order to guarantee the availability of the programs and functions. In this way, two areas were effectively tied to each other, which had to fulfill different objectives.

With the emergence of the DevOps movement, approaches were sought as to how this conflict of goals could be overcome and thus the maximum customer benefit from both areas could be realized, so to speak. In this context, a wide variety of techniques were evaluated and in some cases newly developed. In addition, measures were also taken to support communication and collaboration between development (Dev) and operations (Ops) and to break down the silo mentality of the two areas.

The benefits of DevOps

Building a culture of shared responsibility, transparency, and faster feedback is the foundation of any high-performing DevOps team. Key success factors for realizing maximum benefits with DevOps are establishing a culture of collaboration and joint problem solving.

Teams that work in silos often don't adhere to the systems that DevOps advocates.

What is required is a systems thinking approach that is aware that actions not only affect one's own team, but also all other teams involved in the release process. For this, transparency and collaboration to achieve jointly pursued goals are essential.

The goal of DevOps is to change the mindset, thereby shaping a mindset that allows the development process to be viewed holistically and breaks down the barrier between development and operations.

In addition to the goal of building greater stability, the focus is also always on the goal of faster delivery of business value. To achieve this, a high level of automation is required. The lack of automated test and review cycles slows release to production, while poor incident response time impacts speed and confidence in teams. With tools that drive automation and new processes, teams can increase productivity and release more frequently with fewer issues.

In addition to the speed at which new solutions and solution parts are made available, systematic incorporation of feedback and rapid response to it is also crucial. Full transparency and seamless communication enable DevOps teams to minimize downtime and resolve issues faster.

If critical issues cannot be resolved quickly, customer satisfaction and trust will decline. In the absence of open communication, important issues may be lost, leading to increased tension and frustration among teams. Open communication both between the teams involved and their members, as well as with stakeholders, helps development and operations teams resolve issues, resolve incidents, and release pipeline faster.

Unplanned work is a reality that every team faces and has a significant impact on team productivity. The existence of suitable processes and a clear prioritization of work can help to handle corresponding incidents more efficiently and to have more time available again for the core tasks of the teams. In this context, it is necessary that handover and prioritization are also made transparent across teams so that the departments involved can anticipate situations and thus act more quickly and in a more targeted manner.

Teams that use DevOps practices consistently deliver better quality to their customers. The increased use of automation and cross-functional collaboration reduces errors, which in turn has a positive impact on recovery times and delivery times.

DevOps culture

DevOps is an agile approach to organizational change that aims to bridge traditional, isolated divides (silo thinking) between teams and establish new processes that enable better collaboration. DevOps leverages various tools and agile engineering practices; however, these are not enough to reap the benefits of DevOps. Without the right mindset and culture, the full benefits of DevOps cannot be realized.

The DevOps culture promotes closer collaboration and shared responsibility between development and operations for the products that are created and maintained. Optimization of the entire value chain and thus the benefit for the customer is at the heart of the effort.

DevOps strives to create multidisciplinary teams that are responsible for the entire lifecycle of a product. These work autonomously and rely on frameworks that equate the importance of operational requirements to that of architecture, design and development.

Prerequisites for a vibrant DevOps culture are increased transparency, communication and collaboration between teams that traditionally work in silos. In the process, important cultural changes must take place to bring these teams closer together. DevOps is an organizational culture shift that emphasizes continuous learning and continuous improvement. This is enabled by team autonomy, rapid feedback, high empathy, and cross-team collaboration.

In order for DevOps to work, a culture of collaboration and shared accountability for commonly held and aspired goals is necessary. This requires a mutual understanding of the work performance, the contribution to the value chain realized by other team members and especially by the other teams involved in the value chain, and their importance for the overall success and the realization of benefits for the customer.

Autonomous teams are another important aspect of DevOps. For development and operations teams to collaborate effectively, they must make decisions and implement changes without a cumbersome and lengthy approval process. This requires handing over trust to teams and creating an environment where there is no fear of making mistakes. This requires clear agreements and understandings about decision-making authority and competencies.

A DevOps team culture values rapid feedback. This contributes to the continuous improvement of a unified development and operations team. For this, it is necessary that there is an awareness that all those involved are moving along a development path (this does not mean a software development path) that demands continuous improvement for each individual as well as for the respective teams as a whole. The prerequisite for this is not to reject errors as blemishes, but to perceive them as opportunities for change and improvement. This is strongly linked to a positive error culture.

Automation is critical to the DevOps culture because it enables great collaboration and frees up resources. By automating and integrating the processes between software development and IT teams, they can create, test and release software faster and more reliably. In addition, much higher qualities can be achieved through automation of tests, for example, than through purely manual testing, since each new development step can be evaluated again and again with the existing test scenarios and thus errors can be detected and fixed very early, often daily or even faster - which not only means a reduction in the time spent on testing and repair, but also frees up more capacity for more value-adding work for the customer through fewer errors occurring.

Basic DevOps procedures

Just as there is no single doctrine on what DevOps is, there is of course also no fixed assignment of certain procedures and methods to DevOps. Nevertheless, there is something like common sense about some procedures and approaches in terms of their importance for successful DevOps implementation. It should be noted that the approaches mentioned are not DevOps inventions, but in some cases were used decades before DevOps was first mentioned. Separate books have been published on each of the topics mentioned. Since the procedures of DevOps are not the focus of this publication, but are only intended as an introduction to the topic, I recommend that you read specialized literature on the topics mentioned if you need or are interested. The following lines represent a selection:

- "Voice of the Customer"

The realization of customer value and the consideration of value from the customer's perspective are at the heart of many agile approaches, especially also in the context of Lean Thinking. By VoC, we mean the process of capturing the customer's expectations, likes, and dislikes in order to identify expressed and unexpressed customer desires.

- Relationship Management

    Knowledge of the various stakeholders and their interests, as well as active management of communication with them, are key success factors for any form of collaboration with (internal or external) customers.

- Lean Process Optimization

    We can define Lean as a system for developing process improvements that is continuous and focused on reducing and eliminating waste.

- Value Stream Mapping

    Value Stream Mapping is a lean management method for analyzing the current state and designing a future state for the series of events that a product or service will go through from the beginning of the specific process to the customer. A Value Stream Map is a visual tool that shows all the critical steps in a specific process and visualizes the associated metrics. It shows the flow of materials and information throughout the process.

- Knowledge Management

    To simplify communication and understanding between Dev and Ops, it is necessary that both parts share relevant knowledge. In this way, experience from operations in turn flows to development, and experience from the development process is available to operations. The use of shared systems, which are also managed and maintained jointly, has proven successful.

- Visual Management

The visualization of processes and individual work packages is an important prerequisite for a common perception of the process and is in the context of the required transparency. Visualization not only provides an ongoing overview of where work packages are currently located, but also of where bottlenecks are located in the process, for example, which need to be addressed.

- Scrum

Scrum is generally known as a framework for agile product development. Not only does it fit very well into the context of DevOps with its values and procedures, but in many cases it is also the first step towards DevOps: When Scrum users realize that they have now optimized the development process with Scrum, the next consideration is often what could now be done with Operations to achieve holistic benefits.

- Shift Left Testing

The approach is very simple: the earlier testing takes place, the faster it is possible to react and the less effort is required to correct errors. Shift Left Testing stands for the fact that the testing process does not start after implementation, but is already understood as part of the development process and the focus is not only on detecting errors, but especially on preventing their occurrence.

- Change Control

In the context of IT, we understand change control to be a (formal or informal) process for ensuring that changes to a product or system are made in a controlled and coordinated manner. Change control reduces the risk of unnecessary changes or errors being introduced into the system. Change control objectives typically include minimal disruption of services, reduction of back-out activities, and cost-effective use of resources required to implement changes. Change control is organized into processes in the context of service management approaches.

- Service Configuration Management

Service Configuration Management is an approach introduced in ITIL- version 2 that tracks all individual configuration items (CI) in an IT system. The system can be a single server or an entire IT department. In large organizations, a configuration manager may be appointed to oversee and manage the process. Service configuration management traditionally consists of planning, identification, control, monitoring and review.

- Release & Deployment Management

Release and Deployment Management aims to plan and control releases (the transfer of products to a test or live environment). On the one hand, this involves ensuring that the right components are released and, on the other, preventing possible negative effects on the live environment.

- Incident Management

Incident management encompasses the entire organizational and technical process of responding to identified or suspected security incidents or operational disruptions. This also includes preparatory measures and processes. The goal of incident management is always to restore service performance as quickly as possible, even if this is done temporarily through workarounds.

- Problem Management

Problem management is the process responsible for managing all problems that occur or could occur in an IT service throughout their lifecycle. The main goals of problem management are to prevent problems and resulting incidents, eliminate recurring incidents, and minimize the impact of incidents that cannot be prevented.

- Kaizen

Kaizen (改善) is the Chinese-Japanese word for "improvement". It refers to the approach of continuous improvement of business processes at all levels and to processes throughout the supply chain. It is usually located in the context of the Toyota production process and lean manufacturing, but has long been used in a wide variety of approaches. It is not a one-time measure, but a continuous process.

- Antifragility

Antifragility is a concept based on the book of the same name by Nassim Nicholas Taleb. Wikipedia describes the concept as follows:
"Under the concept of antifragility, Taleb extends his observations and insights about unpredictable events to broad areas of life, for example, evolution, politics, economics, culture, technological innovation, health, education.
Taleb uses the term antifragility to encompass and describe the general phenomenon that, in the face of volatility and the various forms of uncertainty, productive and positive developments also occur - and not just negative and destructive ones. Thus, antifragility is generally the quality or ability to improve under uncertainty, variability, disruption, and stress. Antifragility is defined as the opposite of fragility in terms of these consequences of being exposed to a changing and unpredictable environment. Fragile suffers under the influence of randomness, variability, disturbance, and stress; it deteriorates or perishes. Antifragile, on the other hand, gains under the same influence; it gets 'better', while robust is merely unaffected by it and remains 'unchanged'.
Taleb describes a triad ("three-scheme") fragile-robust-antifragile. Antifragility is not absolute, but always given up to a certain degree of intensity of change or disturbance and, moreover, observer-related.

The property of antifragility can be observed and described above all in the realm of the living and social (and thus also including the economy). The survival of institutions such as banks or political institutions thus depends on their degree of fragility or antifragility.

In the face of uncertainty and insecurity, decisions can thus be made on the basis of the criterion of whether something can be regarded as (rather) fragile or (rather) antifragile. There is no need to resort to forecasts or predictions. Precise forecasts in the field of the social and living are not possible (or only to a very limited extent) due to incomplete knowledge.

Antifragility generally manifests itself in overcompensation and overreaction to disruptions and stress, often leading to a better outcome than expected or feared. These findings have been summarized in proverbs since at least ancient times, e.g. ingenium mala saepe movent (Latin "adversity awakens the mind"), When life gives you a lemon, make lemonade (English "When life gives you a lemon, make lemonade out of it", necessity is the mother of invention). This includes post-traumatic growth or the observation that attention and concentration on something, for example an oral lecture or a written text, increase in an unsettled and noisy environment. This always applies only up to a certain degree of disturbance.

An example of the observation of antifragility in the biological realm is the observation by the Berlin surgeon Julius Wolff (1836-1902) that bones become denser with episodic loading and degrade when they are not loaded (Wolff's law). Accordingly, lack of load due to little exercise and long periods of rest and the accompanying decline in bone density can also be a reason - and not exclusively the consequence - of aging processes.[1]"

---

[1] Wikipedia.com (Accessed 11-2020)

TWO
Continuous ...

Continuous Integration, Continuous Delivery and Continuous Deployment are three concepts that optimally support DevOps and the associated concern of automating processes. However, it seems that the three terms are not really comprehensible to everyone who uses them in the discussion, and it is not uncommon for the three terms to be used synonymously or even confused. It therefore makes sense to present the three terms more precisely in this context and to distinguish them from one another.

Continuous Integration is the first step

In continuous integration, a code change that is implemented and marked complete by the developer is committed to a remote repository. This triggers a process in which the new, changed code is run in its entirety through a series of automated tests on a server. These tests, including regression tests, ensure that - while new functionality has been added - no existing functionality has been lost.

Best practice is gated commits. This involves testing one person's newly created code before sharing it with other developers or testers. This encourages small changes that are frequently merged. Changes are thus straightforward and the status of the software continuously improves as the new code is tested and any issues identified can be quickly addressed.

Continuous integration means that new code is deployed frequently, which in most cases triggers automated testing. This is the prerequisite for Continuous Delivery and Continuous Deployment.

Continuous Delivery und Continuous Deployment

The two terms are not clearly defined and are sometimes confused with each other. If we assume Continuous Integration, this process is usually followed by automated tests, followed by a staging environment, from which the solution is finally transferred to the production level. In most cases, a distinction is now made between Continuous Delivery and Continuous Deployment directly in this process step. While in the context of Continuous Delivery the impulse for delivery is set manually, in the context of Continuous Deployment it is part of the automated process. So in the former context there is still human control, at least in theory, whereas in the latter the process triggers the delivery process independently when all programmed prerequisites are met.

THREE
WHAT IS DEVOPS LEADERSHIP?

The concept of leadership has changed continuously over the past decades. On the one hand, this is due to changes in the people who lead, but on the other hand, it is also due to changes in the framework conditions and self-perception of the people who are led.

While leadership was long characterized by hierarchy and a certain understanding of class, this has since changed. My image of the earlier idea of leadership is that of a commander who sends his troops into battle on the commander's mound and - while watching this "spectacle" - enjoys a glass of wine. Today, leadership is understood completely differently.

In recent decades, the term "leadership" has become associated with "management" in many contexts. However, this is in no way the same thing: If management is essentially about administering what exists and cultivating and maintaining existing spheres of influence, a leader is a person who inspires, motivates and enthuses others through his or her personal example, and often leads and leads the way himself or herself.

Transformational leadership

In the context of DevOps, we need leaders who have a vision and embrace change. The 2017 State of DevOps Report[1] describes the type of leadership needed as follows:

"Transformational leadership is a model in which leaders inspire and motivate followers to achieve higher levels of performance by bringing their values and purpose into play, facilitating broad change in the organization."

The concept of transformational leadership goes back to the book "Leadership" published by James McGregor Burns in 1978. In it, he defines transformational leadership as a process in which leaders and their followers bring each other to higher levels of morale and motivation. This statement encompasses a fundamental shift in focus. It posits that leadership involves not only an approach to changing the morale and motivation of subordinates, but that it should also affect the leader in the same way. This means that the change lies in the entire system of leadership and all those involved in it: the led and the leader.

Even today, more than 40 years after the publication of the book "Leadership," the concept of transformational leadership is, in the opinion of many experts, one of the most important works on the subject of leadership. In this context, a four-stage process model has proven its worth:

1. Creating an inspiring vision for the future
2. De Build and support people's motivation to engage with the vision.
3. The control of the implementation of the vision
4. Building and strengthening the relationship with employees

Of course, this also requires a certain personality. The State of DevOps Report from 2017, which I mentioned earlier, identifies five characteristics of the work of a transformational leader:

- Vision
- Inspiring communication
- Intellectual stimulation
- Supporting leadership
- Personal recognition

5-step leadership model

This leadership model undoubtedly presupposes a certain conception of "team" in which the latter is assumed to be self-motivated and committed to the common task or mission. The necessary framework and support in the form of "coaching" are important prerequisites. It is important to understand that in an organization leadership takes place on a wide variety of levels. In his book "Level 5 Leadership: Good to Great", Jim Collins describes five levels of leadership, whereby the various levels are all important and necessary for overall success:

- Level 1 - A capable individual: This describes experts in specific fields who are knowledgeable in their field and know and can apply theories and practices in their field. However, these are often individualists who are not necessarily team players.
- Level 2 - Contributing Team Member: They can also be described as experts in their field, but in doing so, they also used their skills to achieve group goals and succeed together with their group.
- Level 3 - Competent Manager: A person who organizes people and resources to achieve predefined goals efficiently and effectively, while controlling that the set course is followed.
- Level 4 - Effective Leader: Shapes a vision and ensures that the team creates work that is aligned with the realization of the vision. This includes inspiring the team and supporting them in achieving progress. Effective leaders often have great influence internally as well as externally.
- Level 5 - Leadership: They lead through their human values, guide companies to real greatness and develop them further. They establish a sustainable organizational culture, which is not dependent on them and their personal characteristics, and also invest in integrating other people into leadership, thus also ensuring sustainable growth and development.

Three different basic types exist among 4th and 5th level managers:

- Leaders who attract and consume followers: they attract followers and use them as resources and tools, but see them as a means to an end and drop them when they no longer provide value.
- Leaders who attract and develop followers: they provide their followers with opportunities for advancement and growth, but always keep them in a dependent position, which they can influence and determine.
- Leaders who attract and develop other leaders: they have an impact beyond their own tenure. Successful lean leaders fall into this category. They lead with questions rather than answers. They understand that leading by answers makes others dependent, whereas leading by questions leads to people developing, searching for and finding answers themselves, thus creating self-organization and, in the long term, a culture of self-direction.

This (lean) leadership understanding is what we also want and use in the context of DevOps.

A central concern for leadership in the DevOps context is the support and implementation of a change process toward the values and approaches used in the DevOps context.

---

[1] _Quelle: https://puppet.com/resources/whitepaper/state-of-devops-report

FOUR
Change according to Lewin and the continuous improvement

There are different models for the representation and implementation of a change process in an organization. While the 8-step process according to John Kotter has become increasingly important and well-known in recent years, there are various other process models which can be applied in the same way in our context.

A model that is convincing in this context due to its simple and pragmatic approach is that of Kurt Lewin, which is based on three phases. The phases are summarized under the following three keywords:

- Unfreeze → Define the current situation / state, design a vision for the desired end state and identify the forces that promote or resist change.

- Change → People are guided through the change. In this process, planned changes are implemented according to a specific plan, thus involving people and turning them into participants. An experimental approach is explicitly possible. The inclusion of people with a role model function can support the process.
- Freezing (refreezing) → New ways of working are established. Ensuring that people do not fall back into old ways of doing things. Positive changes and implementation of the new behaviors are rewarded.

Unfreeze

The unfreezing phase is also described by Lewin as "overcoming inertia". Lewin describes three steps for this:

1. Clear presentation of the current situation. This is done to the advantage of the cooperation of the people involved and leads to the fact that the participants have a deeper identification with the problem and thus a more comprehensive picture of the situation can be presented.
2. Creating a vision of the desired target state. The following applies: The more detailed, colorful and attractive the vision is, the more likely people are to get involved in order to implement this vision.
3. Identification of forces that will hinder or promote implementation. Here, the use of classic measures from stakeholder management makes sense.

Change (Change)

The challenge of change is not so much creating a meaningful and purposeful plan, but rather taking the steps to bring the people involved and affected along on the journey and approaching change with them. Change always means a potential threat to those affected. "What will change for me?" - "Do I even have a place in the new organization / state?" - "What will I get out of it?". The process must be carefully planned and accompanied. Fears must be taken seriously and addressed, enthusiasm and excitement must be channeled. If it is not possible to convince those involved, there is a great risk in growing resistance, which may slow down the process or even bring it to a standstill.

Freezing (Refreezing)

Once the target state formulated in the vision has been achieved, the system is often still in a very unstable state for quite some time. Old behaviors and ideas emerge and only if it is possible to counter these impulses and consciously turn away from them can what has been achieved be stabilized and the new desired processes and measures can be implemented sustainably. It can be useful to create incentive systems for this purpose, which reward desired procedures and identify old, no longer desired ones and present them as such.

FIVE
Steps for the introduction and optimization of DevOps

If we now approach the transformation process in the direction of DevOps based on Lewis' process, this results in a number of challenges which can be mastered with a suitable approach.

Unfreezing - the need for change

In general, we face four key challenges when thinking about deploying DevOps in an organization. These are:

- Silo mentality: Many organizations consist of individual silos, which behave like individual organizations and are only focused on the silo world. As a result, however, this quickly loses the actual raison d'être of the customer. A customer can be a paying client in a company or a resident, for example, in the context of municipal organizations. The customer is not interested in the silos, but in having his value added and his benefit provided by his supplier. If a silo mentality is now built up, the focus on this purpose is lost and it is essentially about self-employment and

the achievement of one's own goals, irrespective of the extent to which these are of importance and benefit in the overall context of the organization and in the service of the customer.
- Wall of confusion: Different issues are important in the two silos "Dev" (development) and "Ops" (operations). Development is measured by its ability to quickly deliver new functionality and changes, while Operations strives for stability and secure processes. Changes mean a risk, which should be avoided as far as possible. Due to these different objectives, communication and understanding of each other's concerns is difficult.
- Local optimizations: If optimizations are not considered and implemented in the context of the entire value creation process, local adjustments tend to result, which in turn may lead to adjustments that do not make sense in another context. This leads to less performant and beneficial processes overall and a potential deterioration of the value creation capability of the process chain for the customer. Instead of deploying resources where they would be most beneficial to the overall process, local budgets are deployed locally. The focus is often not on the benefits for the customer, but on the local needs and demands of the local areas.
- Waste in processes: Local optimization and silo thinking lead to waste due to bureaucracy and interface problems. Time, performance, resources and energy are wasted.

While such developments were of minor importance for a long time, as many companies could be relatively secure in local markets, today's technological and societal developments lead to challenges that can also become threatening for large organizations and force them to act.

The emergence and establishment of cloud technology has meant that even small companies and start-ups can suddenly access computing power and storage space that previously could only be operated by large corporations. Instead of building and operating IT infrastructure, it can be obtained from the network on a usage basis and deployed globally. This also creates a new market situation. Where once only geographically close organizations were competitors in offerings, customers can now source globally and providers can offer globally. An ever-increasing degree of automation is available due to the almost inexhaustible computing power and makes it possible to submit offers that previously could only be delivered by corporations with thousands of employees. This results in competitive situations that can no longer be controlled and defeated by the company's own size, market power, financial framework conditions or the like, and a corresponding need for action with regard to the company's own organization and its processes.

In his 2004 book "Does IT Matter," Nicolas Carr described the way in which the introduction of new technologies takes shape. He identified three stages:

- Innovation: Organizations introduce new technologies because they expect to benefit from them.
- Maturity: New technologies will increasingly be used in exactly the same way by market competitors. The differentiation factor is increasingly falling away.
- Expediency: The technologies used become the standard and are taken for granted by the market. Their use is commercialized to such an extent that standard products and offerings develop and it makes more sense to use a standard product than to further develop one's own.

We also find this situation with regard to technologies as they are used in the context of DevOps. Cloud computing, automations, etc. have long since ceased to be the differentiating feature of a few, but have become indispensable in many industries and areas of life. Organizations have to come to terms with corresponding approaches if they want to survive on the market. This leads to a standardization of offers and services, which provides a basis for innovations in the core area of the organization.

Once an organization has understood the need for change, the next step is to develop a shared vision of what needs to be achieved. It is not enough to decide not to continue with the existing or to want to change. Rather, a common goal must be defined. This is generally a process that takes place in several steps:

1. Creating a shared vision: A representation of what the organization wants to achieve in the future. A vision should be attractive and motivate stakeholders to implement/realize it. All further measures and activities are measured against whether they support the realization of the vision.
2. Formulating a Mission: An organization's mission is often expressed in the form of a mission statement. It reflects an organization's desires and intentions and focuses on presenting and communicating a shared understanding of the organization's course and purpose.
3. Definition of business objectives. These follow from the vision and mission, but are formulated in concrete terms and often follow the requirements of the "SMART" pattern (Specific - Measurable - Achievable - Reasonable - Time-Bound).

In order to develop awareness of the need for change, it makes sense to work out this change together with those affected and also to determine vision, mission and goals together (or if this is not possible, to concretize these together for one's own actions and activities).

A clear change vision is described by John Kotter as a central success factor of any change process. He names three central purposes for this:

- Clarification: Ensures that everyone has a common understanding of the direction and goal of the change process. Ensures that all stakeholders have the same idea of the direction and understand and support its necessity.

- Motivation: Change almost always means pain or difficulty. Habitual and familiar ways of doing things must be shed and new, unfamiliar and possibly dangerous or unappealing paths are taken. *"A good vision for change helps remove the natural resistance to what is necessary (often painful) by being hopeful and motivating."* [1]
- Coordination: An understood and shared vision gives people at different levels of the hierarchy the opportunity to align their work and decisions to it, and thus work to implement the shared vision without the need for ongoing decisions from leadership on detailed issues.

Change - plan and approach the transformation

To understand leadership in the context of DevOps, it is necessary to understand how a transformation to DevOps works in organizations in general. It is important to understand that there is no blueprint that can be imposed on virtually any organization. It is also not expedient to buy the corresponding processes from a consulting firm as a kind of manual. Rather, the process itself should be understood as an agile change process in the form of conducting experiments in which steps are taken in the direction of the vision, reviewed, and adjusted if necessary. In concrete terms, this could look like this:

The organization decides to implement specific procedures in certain teams that are of fundamental importance for DevOps, e.g., an implementation of Scrum in the development area, a visualization of the value creation processes, or the introduction of tools for process automation (e.g., in testing). These first steps are implemented as a test case, optimized and adapted as required.

Often, these first steps are not strategically planned, but initiated by the employees themselves. This offers the opportunity to try out new approaches and gain experience. In any case, however, there should also be a clear idea of what is to be achieved with the experiment.

The rollout should continue to be incremental and iterative from these initial activities. Incremental means that experiments and measures are coordinated and perceived and evaluated in terms of a more holistic goal. Iterative means that we have a development process, which in this case is less about the product than the process itself. What has been achieved is regularly reviewed in relation to the agreed goals, and from this, in turn, further measures and steps are derived and addressed.

This approach not only promotes a process-related transformation, but in many cases also a cultural transformation and, if the team is involved in or leads the process, a change in the team's self-perception and identification with the desired goal. Such changes quickly radiate beyond the team(s) directly involved and also lead to changes in a larger context up to the boundaries of the organization and possibly even beyond.

It is precisely in this phase of transformation that different speeds of change often exist within an organization. In this context, the term "bimodal IT" is sometimes used. This can make perfect sense as a step toward implementing new conditions, since different areas may have different prerequisites or may already be closer to the target state (or may no longer require transformation). It therefore makes perfect sense to consider and carry out the transformation requirements for individual areas on an individual basis to ensure that no area is overburdened, but that everyone makes progress in the transformation within the scope of their capabilities and goals.

In doing so, it is important to avoid excessive divergence within IT. If deviations exist for too long or become permanent, a dysfunctional structure can develop that creates a harmful divergence in the culture.

In the agile context, there is a concept of spreading experience and knowledge gained, which is known as "dividing and sowing". The idea here is that acquired knowledge and experience do not have to be made over and over again by different teams, or that they are only passed on via narrative/communication. For this reason, it has proven successful to split up teams that have successfully undergone a transformation and to make them the nucleus of two new teams that already have the corresponding experience in the team, which can support a transfer in the new team. This approach, which is also used successfully in the introduction of Scrum, for example, can also be used in our context.

Once a sufficient basis has been achieved, the next step is an organization-wide roll-out. In this phase, too, it is necessary for success to include the circumstances of different areas in the planning. It is possible that there will be setbacks during the implementation process, or that different phases will overlap. However, it is important to see further, closer integration of the overall organization as a process goal. Within the framework of this process, however, it is not a matter of imposing what has been learned in the individual teams on the entire organization. Rather, continuous learning within the framework of an iterative procedure will also be necessary within the framework of this process. Overall, this process should also convey the realization that it is not about cementing a final status, but rather that the "new way of working" requires continuous further development, based on experiments and their evaluation, and will become the standard, so to speak.

Stakeholder management

A key success factor for any change process is knowing the relevant stakeholders and their interests. A stakeholder is any person or group that may be affected by or have an impact on the change. This includes the leadership and team implementing the process, the potential stakeholders and affected parties, others who may benefit, and those who may be negatively impacted.

The stakeholder management process is described and subdivided differently by various authors. The procedure is usually relatively similar, often only the division of the individual phases varies. In our context, we want to start from the following procedure:

1. Stakeholder identification
2. Categorize stakeholders
3. Analyze stakeholder needs
4. Set goals to meet the needs
5. Perform and monitor stakeholder management and take corrective action as necessary.

Stakeholder identification

When it comes to identifying stakeholders, the challenge quickly arises that, depending on the project, there is a very large number of people who need to be considered, partly as individuals and partly as parts of groups. Depending on the project, these include, for example:

- Employees (if necessary to be differentiated according to different teams / departments / hierarchy levels / interests in the project)
- Internal and external departments (HR, administration, GL ...)
- External entities involved in the affected processes (suppliers, customers, infrastructure operators, marketing partners, other business units outside the actual organization)
- Governmental or public institutions, industry organizations, employee representation, which are to be involved, either through the definition of laws or guidelines or through a possible direct influence.
- Professional or regulatory, internal or, if applicable, also commissioned organizations, e.g. data protection, information security.

Individuals may be part of multiple groups in different capacities and may be involved multiple times accordingly.

Categorization of stakeholders

In the context of stakeholder categorization, there may be different viewpoints and levels that need to be considered:

- Power and influence on the project and the corresponding environment
- Interests or attitude towards the project (rejecting, supporting, takes advantage of the project, has/fears disadvantages due to the project ...)
- Subdivision into stakeholders who are only informed and those who are also actively involved or who may even have a special role in the process.

In this context, it is possible that certain stakeholders may change both their importance and their level of interest or the nature of their involvement during the project, for example, when certain phases are completed or others are included.

Analyze stakeholder needs and set goals

Particularly with regard to the involvement of stakeholders, it is important to prepare careful planning which, on the one hand, is suitable for keeping the stakeholders in the project's favor and potentially being able to count on their support. In addition, however, it is also important to record and plan how the cooperation and information policy will be planned, controlled, monitored and, if necessary, corrected during the course of the project. In addition to planning the individual activities and measures, this always includes determining who will take care of them, whereby the tasks can be distributed among several people and groups. Analysis and goal setting are closely linked, but may not necessarily be carried out by the same people.

Perform and monitor - take corrective action if necessary.

The measures are implemented by the responsible persons and departments and monitored within the framework of the project in order to be able to take immediate corrective action in the event of undesirable developments or errors.

Change - framework conditions, concepts and measures

If we want to plan change, it makes sense to start by looking at some helpful concepts and measures that will allow us to make decisions more purposefully and to benefit from the experience and discovery of others, rather than having to work everything out ourselves. Of course, this is not to say that planning and implementing our own experiments and applying what we have learned through them would not be of paramount importance in the context of goal-directed advancement. Nevertheless, knowledge of existing approaches and thought patterns can help to develop new and better solutions and, ideally, to better assess the possible effects of measures even before they are implemented.

Corporate culture - the foundation

R. Westrum in his article "A typology of organizational cultures" described [2] three different ways in which organizations process information. He named these:

- Pathological

Organizations with a pathological corporate culture function in a power-oriented manner. Responsibility is shunned and cooperation is not perceived as goal-oriented. Rather, the focus is on asserting oneself and one's interests. There is virtually no culture of error. The mistakes of others are perceived as an opportunity for self-profiling. Accordingly, it is important to find and name scapegoats. Further development and new approaches are perceived as a risk that can lead to personal relegation. Accordingly, changes are blocked, and if they should be unavoidable, everything is done to avoid being suspected of complicity in the event of failure.

- Bureaucratic

Bureaucratic organizations are primarily rule-oriented. Cooperation is possible, but only within the framework of the regulated measure. Where there is no rule, there is no way. Own responsibility is negated - the rules are responsible and the individual is only their user. People who tackle changes are not hindered, but are seen as rather suspect; there is no rule "yet". When mistakes happen, justice is sought and change is initially perceived as a disruption of the existing order and structures.

- Generative

A generative corporate culture is performance-oriented. The organization is understood as a system based on the cooperation of its parts. Bridge builders between different topics, areas and departments are perceived as correspondingly important. They help to make the system as a whole more stable and efficient, thus contributing to its growth and success. In the same way, errors are also perceived as the basis for development and as an important step within the framework of development. Risk management is actively pursued, and errors are not covered up, but perceived as triggers for change and learning.

If we want to be successful with agile methods - and among them especially with DevOps - a generative organizational culture is a central prerequisite. If this does not exist, we must first work to achieve it. The leadership's role model function is of central importance here. This is not about lip service or marketing measures, but about what is exemplified in everyday working life. Where appropriate developments are hindered or thwarted, only clear intervention by management will bring success, willy-nilly. Pathological or bureaucratic corporate cultures also promote silo thinking and prevent systems thinking. In this way, they pursue an objective that runs counter to the goals of a DevOps implementation.

Cross-functional self-organized teams

The central success factor of all agile frameworks and methods is the formation and use of cross-functional, self-organized and motivated teams. Many agile initiatives fail or come to nothing because organizations take too little account of this fact and prefer to focus on the methods and tools of a framework instead of changing the organization with its structures and culture so that teams are optimally supported and promoted in their activities.

Let's compare an agile team with a sports team. Although there may well be particularly talented specialists in such teams, a team wins or loses as a whole and a club, its management and its coaches will only be successful if the team is motivated on the pitch, wants to win and is fully committed to doing so. To do this, the teams must have skills and knowledge at their disposal, or they must be supported in their development and expansion. To do this, the club may invest in infrastructure, training materials and specialists who teach the team special skills and techniques. However, an experienced club president knows that all these measures will only lead to success in competition if one succeeds in ensuring the team's motivation and will to win, and one provides the team with framework conditions, be it technical as well as emotional and social, that support the team in winning. If this does not happen, you can really only hope that the opposing team is "even weaker".

This is exactly the same with regard to agile teams in the context of DevOps or other agile practices and frameworks. It is necessary to first work on the framework conditions. Hierarchical structures with a high pressure to justify themselves and a focus on position and standing cannot be the right environment for an agile team. But also within such a team a situation should be created which is not influenced by hierarchies or positions. Rather, the basis of a cross-functional, self-organized team is an inner freedom from hierarchy, which is characterized by the fact that each team member contributes equally within the framework of his or her knowledge and skills and thus becomes an equal co-creator of the team product. He or she contributes his or her experience and exchanges ideas with colleagues. Decisions are not made by hierarchy, but after examining the options in favor of the best possible options for the (process) customer. The prerequisite for this is communication and cooperation, focused on a common goal.

However, this very goal is critical to the team's success. A commonly understood and shared team leads to focusing the power and actions of the team with regard to a common point. Of course, this should be important in terms of a common understanding of what the goal is, on the one hand, but also in terms of team composition (people who can identify with the goal to be achieved), on the other.

An agile team and its environment

When we talk about teams in the agile context, it makes sense to clarify what distinguishes teams from a group of people working more or less randomly on a project or product, because often companies pay too little attention to this.

When we talk about teams, it makes sense to include the research of Bruce Wayne Tuckman (1938-2016), an American psychologist. Tuckman first presented _research results[3] in 1965 regarding the development of teams, which are known to many people under the keywords "Forming - Storming - Norming - Performing" and partly still "Adjourning". Briefly summarized, it is about the following:

Forming

The forming phase includes the elements of orientation and getting to know each other. Uncertainty is high in this phase and people look for leadership and authority. A member who asserts authority or has knowledge can take control. Team members ask questions like, "What does the team offer me?" - "What is expected of me?" - "Will I fit into the team?" Most interactions are social as members get to know each other. This phase is essential precisely as a foundation for team development. If it does not take place, or if it is not possible, for example, due to the size of the team, external pressure or external influences such as working in virtual, distributed teams, this generally has a negative impact on the development of the team, the perception of it as a team and, based on this, on the quality of communication and collaboration in later phases, which of course also has an impact on the quality of the services provided.

Storming

The Storming phase is the most difficult and critical phase. It is a time marked by conflict and competition as individual strong personalities emerge. Team performance usually declines during this phase as energy is expended on unproductive activities. Members may disagree on team goals, and subgroups and cliques may form around strong personalities or areas of agreement. In cases of close collaboration, aligning handoffs and interfaces among team members can be a major challenge. Often, those involved retreat to their background of experience and insist on doing things the way they have always done them and perceived them to be right. To overcome this phase, members must work to overcome obstacles, accept individual differences, and work through conflicting ideas about team tasks and goals. Teams can get stuck in this phase. If conflicts are not addressed, this can lead to long-term problems. In the agile context, it is precisely here that support from non-involved third parties such as agile coaches or, in Scrum, a Scrum Master, is important to support communication and bring alignment on a common goal to the forefront.

Norming

When teams get through the Storming phase, conflicts are resolved and a degree of unity emerges. In the Norming phase, a consensus develops about how the team works together, what processes and procedures are. Interpersonal differences begin to dissolve and a sense of cohesion and unity emerges. Team performance increases during this phase as members learn to work together and focus on team goals. However, there is always a risk of falling back into the storming phase, especially if issues or differing opinions and ideas have not been addressed beforehand, but have been kept quiet and "swept under the rug" for the sake of peace.

Performing

In the Performing phase, consensus and collaboration are well established and the team is mature, organized, and functioning well. There is a clear and stable structure, and members are committed to the team's mission. When problems and conflicts arise, they are handled constructively. The team is focused on problem solving and achieving team goals. Ideally, a certain "flow" is established in the collaboration. This requires team members to identify with the team and the common goal.

Adjourning

In the adjourning phase, there is usually a stable team that also perceives itself as such. The focus is on completing the final tasks and documenting the effort and results. As the workload is reduced, individual members may be assigned to other teams and the team disbands. There may be regrets when the team ends, so ceremonial recognition of the team's work and success can be helpful.

Teams are successful not only thanks to the knowledge and performance of the people gathered in them, but because they see themselves as a team and are more successful in cooperation through communication and mutual support and joint development of solutions than the individuals involved in the team would be separately. However, the process of team building takes time and involves a certain amount of effort, which is always renewed (sometimes on a larger or smaller scale) when there are changes in the composition of the team. Accordingly, it is important to view teams as a longer-term construct. Various research studies have shown that, depending on the context, teams sometimes only reach full performance after one to two years and only then have they reached their maximum capacity.

If organizations are conspicuous for poor planning or the desire to keep adding specialists to the team on a temporary basis, they permanently prevent the team from being successful and efficient within its capabilities, which has a negative impact on the quality and quantity of the work results. In reality, it has proven much better to view the team as a core group that implements the core tasks of a project and, if necessary, to commission external bodies and to cooperate with them on a temporary basis. In the software context, for example, such external bodies can be architects, external suppliers or platform operators, or experts for certain topics that are only important for a limited period of time, among others.

Teams and their powers

But how should such a team be properly deployed? What framework conditions are important? In his article "The Psychology of Self-Management in Organizations", Harvard professor J. Richard Hackmann [4] presented a layered model of the various forms of authority in teams. We will find that not all of them are equally suitable for use in agile contexts and DevOps.

In most companies, there is a traditional image of leadership. One could speak of a manager-led leadership culture in which the team is tasked with carrying out management's instructions. This means that the knowledge and competence of the team is not perceived, or only to a limited extent. It is based on an understanding of leadership in which the leader is "the knower" and the team is, so to speak, a multiplication of the leader's power of execution. Ideally, "automata" would be used here, which execute the will of their manager. If the leader makes wrong or suboptimal decisions, the team will also follow these largely uncritically, which will potentially have very negative consequences.

Self-organized teams are characterized by the fact that they decide themselves how the agreed work is carried out. Here, the leader is responsible for planning, compilation and general framework conditions, but does not monitor and control the concrete work process, instead leaving it up to the team to decide. This type of collaboration supports agile working methods and DevOps because it helps to promote cooperation and communication and provides the framework for the skills and knowledge of team members to be used in a targeted manner.

Self-directed teams go one step further. Not only do they have the power to decide how to implement tasks that come from the outside, but they also have the power to determine the planning and context themselves. They are autonomous as a team, but they still form a team. The manager only sets the general course here. Depending on how it plays out, this also means that the team decides who is part of the team and who is not, and in what way the team reports on its activities. In the agile context, this approach is very widespread. In particular, this characteristic, which Hackman calls "self-directed", corresponds in large part to what Scrum, for example, understands by "self-organized and self-responsible".

Self-managed teams go one step further. They work outside the context and strategy of their organization. In doing so, they also decide on their own priorities and processes. Such teams - unless they simply owe their existence to a leadership weakness in the organization - are often found in creative and innovative processes. In the context of DevOps and Agile, such teams are not seen as goal-oriented, since in both cases a target set by customers / organization etc. and its implementation is understood as part of the model.

DevOps and the customers

Voice of the Customer

When we talk about processes in this context, we need to take a closer look. On the one hand, we often speak of process customers, i.e., those persons, groups, or areas that further process or use the work results processed in a process step; on the other hand, we also speak of customers in everyday language and mean those people who pay a manufacturer, service provider, or retailer a fee - often in the form of money - in exchange for goods or services.

In this context, it is useful to introduce the term Voice of the Customer. Wikipedia describes this term as follows:

"Voice of the Customer", also mostly referred to as Voice of the Customer (VOC) in German, is a term used in business and information technology (e.g., ITIL) to describe the process of capturing the customer's expectations, likes and dislikes in order to identify expressed and unexpressed customer desires. Voice of the customer also refers to the technique in market research that produces a detailed data set of customer wants and needs, organizes it into a hierarchical structure, and then prioritizes it in terms of relative importance and satisfaction with current alternatives. Voice of the Customer studies typically consist of qualitative and quantitative research steps. They are usually conducted at the beginning of each new product definition. Process or service design initiative to better understand the customer's wants and needs. It serves as a key input for new product definition, quality function definition, and detailed design specification definition.

There are very many ways to gather the information needed, such as focus groups, individual interviews, contextual interviewing, ethnographic techniques, etc. These are a series of structured in-depth interviews that focus on customers' experiences with current products or alternatives within the category under consideration. Needs information is then extracted, organized into a more user-friendly hierarchy, and then prioritized by customers. In addition, customer complaints can also be used as responsive sources.

It is critical that the core product development team be involved in this process from the beginning. They need to be the ones leading the definition of the topic, the design of the sample (i.e., customer types), the generation of questions for the interview guides, the conduct or observation and analysis of the interviews, and the extraction and processing of the needs statements.[5]"

The voice of the customer - his wishes and needs - is of central importance for every process and every process step in the business context. Only by aligning our working methods, processes and products precisely to their needs can we create value for the customer, which ultimately also leads to the customer being willing to pay for the service provided or the product created/offered and thus ensure the financing and survival of the company. This approach from the business world is of course not limited to the processes of commercially oriented companies, but also occurs in the context of organizations under public law or other structures, even if at first glance the relationship of goods/services for money often does not appear quite so transparent.

In particular, it is also the customer who assigns value to offers and services and in doing so also determines the quality criteria which he demands or presupposes in order to acquire a service. A distinction can be made between different levels of quality. On the one hand, there is a level of quality which is virtually taken for granted, and on the other hand, there may be higher quality expectations which serve more as a distinguishing feature and are set in relation to price or other criteria, for example, in the context of an evaluation or purchase decision. Quality expectations are not made explicit in every case, and sometimes the quality criteria expressed and those actually applied differ from one another, which means that close attention must be paid here.

Considering the above aspects, it is obvious that knowing the wishes and ideas of one's customers is a critical success factor, which in turn requires knowing one's customers in the first place and having defined and managing a strategy in terms of customer engagement and interaction.

Business Relationship Management

Relationship management is a strategy in which an organization plans and maintains continuous contact for its target audience. This management can be between an organization and its customers, as well as between an organization and other organizations. Relationship management aims to create a partnership between organizations and individuals, rather than viewing the relationship as a mere transaction.

In this context, relationship management encompasses strategies for building and expanding customer relationships for a company and its offerings, as well as consolidating them. Most frequently, relationship building takes place at the customer level, but also between companies. For this purpose, a company defines specific responsibilities and tasks. Building a customer relationship is beneficial for all parties involved. Consumers who feel that a company is responsive to their needs are likely to continue using that company's products and services.

In practice, a distinction is often made between Customer Relationship Management (CRM) and Business Relationship Management. The former focuses on the business-to-customer area, the latter on the business-to-business area. CRM involves a significant amount of data and sales analysis to understand market trends, the economic landscape, and consumer tastes. CRM can encompass processes from marketing and sales initiation to existing customer support and retention.

Business Relationship Management (BRM) deals with relationships with business partners, suppliers, vendors and their employees. Business Relationship Management (BRM) promotes a positive and productive relationship between a company and its business partners. It focuses on building trust and cooperation, reinforcing rules and expectations, and setting boundaries. It can also help with dispute resolution, contract negotiation and cross-sale opportunities.

DevOps and the processes

The idea of processes and their optimization in DevOps is strongly oriented to the ideas commonly used in the context of Lean Thinking.

Lean Thinking

Lean thinking is an approach that originated in Japanese manufacturing technology, which is used in many industries around the world. Ultimately, it is a mindset that aims to manage work in a lean way. Lean focuses on delivering high customer value through continuous improvement of business processes.

The Lean Thinking concept is more than just using tools or changing some steps in a business process. It is about perceiving and evaluating business processes differently.

Lean has its origins in the automotive industry, particularly in the Toyota Production System. The Japanese company was able to create a sustainable ecosystem for work in which it could minimize its costs, ensure the efficiency of its processes and thus sell its products at a competitive price. This made it easy for Toyota to penetrate new markets (USA/Europe) because their process model allowed them to sell their products significantly cheaper than the local industry.

The basis for this was that the manufacturing process could be accelerated considerably without compromising or limiting quality. Rather, very special attention was paid in the production process to identifying and avoiding any form of waste, as well as the consistent orientation of all activities towards the realization of added value for the customer.

Lean is based on two pillars. They are the necessary foundations for the development of Lean Thinking. They are continuous improvement and respect for people. Lived conviction is this: When employees align their thinking with continuous improvement and respect, they can formulate and execute better business decisions and strategies that positively impact the company's productivity.

Continuous improvement refers to the active pursuit of constantly looking for and implementing ways to improve. Continuous improvement enables teams to identify non-value-added activities in their business operations. This enables them to increase team productivity and deliver value to their end customers faster.

Respect is a central aspect of many agile methodologies and frameworks. If everyone in an organization operated under a system of respect, they would ensure that their efforts were aimed at the best interest of the recipient of their work. Teams that show respect for their customers would not seek activities that do not meet the customer's needs. Instead of relying on their own assumptions, these would be questioned and clarified with the customer, thereby ensuring that resources are focused on satisfying the customer in the best possible way. This ensures that any work the team takes on is valuable to the customer. To ensure that this respect is not just a marketing idea, but is actually lived - and the customer will see this - it must be lived at all levels of the organization.

In an organization that has adapted Lean company-wide, managers trust their employees and give them autonomy to get the job done. This level of trust shown then becomes the impetus for employees to show the same respect and attitude toward their work and, in turn, the company's customers. Employees within a Lean organization show respect to their peers through collaboration, ensuring that work is managed and distributed by the entire team. This allows them to leverage everyone's skills and capacity while striving for faster delivery of quality value to the customer.

James P. Womack and Daniel T. Jones laid out the five basic principles for any lean implementation. These are defining value, understanding the value stream, flow, implementing a pull system, and constantly striving for perfection:

What is value?

A central success factor for any company is a deep understanding of what "value" means to its customers. Only then can it develop products and services that meet its customers' needs. Without a clear understanding of what customers want and need, companies miss the mark. Not only does this mean not being able to give customers what they want, but it also means that companies have spent their time, effort and resources working on something that does not result in value. To know this customer value, it is necessary to know your customers and their needs.

Understanding the value stream

Once it is understood what is of value to the customer, it is a matter of aligning all processes to optimally achieve this value. This means identifying all processes and steps that transform raw materials or ideas into functioning products that customers will use. This is also what value stream means as a lean thinking principle.

Value Stream Mapping is a lean technique that identifies the process by which products and services are created and delivered. The goal is to uncover any steps in the process that do not add value to the final product and then work toward eliminating that waste.

Flow

After the various forms of waste (muda / mura / muri) have been eliminated in the value stream, the flow of the value stream is now focused and optimized. The goal is a smooth flow. This means that the work is not hindered or blocked.

It is not easy to establish a fluid work flow. This can mean introducing changes to the organization that some may initially be resistant to. Cross-functional and cross-functional thinking must be introduced to keep work flowing smoothly. Even the physical environment in which teams work should be organized to encourage collaboration.

Pull system

By eliminating waste and ensuring a smooth workflow, the realization of new products and services is significantly shortened. This is a basic prerequisite for no longer producing products in stockpiles, but realizing them as needed in the sense and for the benefit of the customer and thus achieving both higher customer satisfaction and, on the other hand, having less capital tied up in the form of semi-finished products.

Striving for perfection

If processes have been aligned to realize value for the customer, this is not a one-time act, but requires constant attention to identify potential for improvement. Identifying value, refining the value stream, creating a smooth process, and constantly striving to produce only when needed and in what quantity are all part of a continuous improvement initiative that the entire organization must support. This means that Lean Thinking must be embedded in the corporate culture. In doing so, the quest to improve processes, products and collaboration is endless and never reaches a final point where no more improvement would be useful or possible. This corporate philosophy can be implemented with a Kaizen approach.

DevOps and Scrum

It would go beyond the scope of this book to present the entire Scrum framework. As far as Scrum is already in use, this would be superfluous anyway, and where this is not the case, I advise obtaining specialized literature for it. In this section I would like to limit myself to the presentation of the interfaces and cooperation of Scrum and DevOps.

Scrum, according to its own definition, is a framework that focuses on making products, or as the German edition of the Scrum Guide 2020 puts it:

"Scrum is a lightweight framework that helps people, teams, and organizations generate value through adaptive solutions to complex problems.

In short, Scrum requires that a:e Scrum Master:in fosters an environment in which

1. *a:e Product Owner:in sorts the work for a complex problem into a Product Backlog;*

2. the Scrum Team generates a valuable increment from a selection of this work within a Sprint;
3. the Scrum Team and its stakeholders review the results and adjust them for the next Sprint;
4. these steps are repeated.

Scrum is simple. Try it as is and see if its philosophy, theory, and structure help you achieve goals and create value. The Scrum framework is intentionally incomplete, defining only the parts needed to implement Scrum theory. Scrum is built on the collective intelligence of the people who use it. Rather than giving people detailed instructions, Scrum's rules guide their relationships and interactions.

Various processes, techniques and methods can be used within the framework. Scrum wraps around existing practices or makes them obsolete. Scrum makes visible the relative effectiveness of current management, environment, and work techniques so that improvements can be made."

If we look at the whole thing from a DevOps perspective, we can certainly say that the Scrum framework is used centrally in the context of "Dev". Here, it supports teams in making applications of the greatest possible customer benefit available to the customer within a manageable period of time.

The Scrum team consists of three roles:

- Scrum Master: focus on the process and ensuring the framework and team collaboration.
- Product owner: focus on maximizing value for the customer
- Development Team: Concrete implementation of the requirements with different special competencies and skills, but always responsible as a whole team.

Interaction with the DevOps team can take place in the development team. For this, however, we should first keep in mind how a development team understands itself. The Scrum Guide makes it very clear that there are no sub-teams or special responsibilities within the Scrum team and titles have no place in this team. This is important for the whole to function as a team and not as a group of specialists. No one has the ability to retreat to a specific responsibility or title. Everyone is part of the team and therefore equally responsible for the entire work. Accordingly, the team is focused on becoming stronger as a whole, which also leads to mutual support and thinking in order to advance the development project as a whole. This also leads to mutual learning and understanding, which in turn leads to greater mutual support. A positive development cycle begins.

When the development team operates within or collaborates with a DevOps team, it is necessary to gradually break down the boundaries and silos between the two areas. A common approach to this is a three-phase approach:

1. **Phase: Improved Dev and Ops CollaborationThe**
   existing Dev and Ops silos are restructured to create tightly knit and collaborative teams that share the same goals from both sides. It may also be reviewed to give developers more responsibility for operations to better understand the needs of the operations side, thereby gradually dissolving the boundaries.

2. **Phase: permanently assigned DevOps team**

   In the second phase, permanently assigned DevOps teams are often installed, which are intended to counteract the impulse to continue to maintain silos and act as a kind of nucleus for the emerging cross-functional teams.

3. **Phase: Cross-functional teams**
   Cross-functional teams are formed from representatives of all disciplines. These can be installed as permanent teams or only as project-specific teams. The teams organize themselves adaptively and self-organized.

DevOps and quality assurance

In the context of quality assurance, using some of the techniques from the context of Extreme Programming that are also used in the context of Scrum and other agile methods is a successful approach. We often speak of "Shift Left Testing" in the context of DevOps to represent that testing and other activities associated with ensuring quality must move further forward (left) on the timeline. On the one hand, this leads to a much lower testing effort per se and, most importantly, to the fact that detected problems can be fixed right away before they lead to consequential errors. The actual goal is not to find errors at an early stage, but to prevent their occurrence as far as possible through intensive cooperation between development and quality assurance, which enables immediate reaction and does not lead to the creation of huge test reports. Ideally, testing is even integrated into the creation of requirements, for example, in order to coordinate requirements for tests even before work begins.

Approaches which are used from Extreme Programming in the context of DevOps are for example:

- Test Driven Development
- Continuous Integration
- Pair Programming
- Collaborative Code Ownership

Test-driven development

Test-driven development (TDD), also called test-driven design, is a method of implementing software programming that combines unit testing, programming, and refactoring in the source code.

Test-driven development was introduced as part of Extreme Programming (XP) and is an agile software development methodology.

The steps of the development are turned upside down, so to speak:

Before writing new code, the programmer must first create a failed component test. Then the programmer creates just enough code to meet that requirement. Once the test passes, the programmer can revise the design and make improvements without changing the behavior.

While TDD focuses on programmer interactions at the unit level, there are other popular methods, such as acceptance test-driven development (ATDD) or behavior-driven development (BDD) , that focus on tests that can be understood by customers.

Test-driven development can create high-quality applications in less time than is possible with older methods. For proper implementation of TDD, developers and testers must anticipate exactly how the application and its features will be used in the real world.

By using TDD, defects can be found and corrected faster than with traditional testing methods. The methodical nature of TDD ensures much higher coverage and initial quality than the classic testing process. Since tests are performed from the beginning of the design cycle, the time and money spent on debugging in later phases is minimized.

It should be noted that, as with any method, the end results of TDD are only as good as the tests used, the thoroughness with which they were performed, and the extent to which they mimic the conditions to which users of the final product are exposed.

Continuous integration

Continuous Integration (CI) is a software development practice in which developers merge their changes several times a day. Each merge triggers an automated code build and test sequence that ideally executes in less than 10 minutes. A successful CI build can lead to further phases of continuous delivery.

If a build fails, the CI system blocks the transition to further phases. The team receives a report and quickly fixes the build, usually within minutes.

The use of continuous integration approaches is now standard in all leading software development companies. Working in small iterations makes the software development process predictable and reliable. Developers can iteratively create new features. Product managers can get the right products to market faster. Developers can find bugs quickly and usually fix them before those bugs are discovered by users.

For continuous integration, all developers working on a project must commit to an approach that is consistent with the methodology. Results must be transparently available to all team members, and build status must be reported to developers as they change code. If the main code branch cannot build or pass tests, an alert is usually sent to the entire development team, which should take immediate action to restore the "green" state.

By using smaller steps, we can estimate more accurately and validate more frequently. A shorter feedback loop means more iterations. And it is the number of iterations, not the number of hours invested, that drives learning. Thus, even in environments and situations where not all details are clear at the beginning of the work, successful developments can be driven and continuously improved based on feedback and passed tests.

For development teams, working in long feedback loops is risky because it increases the likelihood of errors and the amount of work required to integrate changes into working software.

Small, controlled changes can occur frequently. By automating all integration steps, developers avoid repetitive work and human error. Instead of deciding when and how to run tests, a CI tool monitors the central code repository and runs all automated tests on each commit. Based on the overall result of the tests, the code commit is either accepted or rejected.

Once we have automatically built and tested our software, it becomes easier to release it. Therefore, Continuous Integration is often extended with Continuous Delivery, a process where code changes are also automatically prepared for a release (CI / CD).

Pair programming

Pair Programming is another technique from the Extremeprogramming framework. It assumes that two heads are better than one and teamwork is effective both in terms of the quality to be achieved and in terms of finding better solutions.

Pair programming is a software development technique of growing importance in which two people work on a single block of code. The programmers take over one of two parts - the driver and the navigator.

The Driver in the process is responsible for carefully writing the code, while the Navigator must review and focus on the action plan.

Numerous studies exist that present the enormous benefits in terms of increased performance and productivity, as well as safe and sound products. However, there are very different opinions on this. My experience shows that the use of pair programming can both reduce implementation quality and error-proneness and increase implementation speed. A very important further benefit lies in the possibility of using such approaches to also simplify the transfer of knowledge and experience by forming pairs of professionals and beginners. Finally, the technique, neatly applied, also helps to strengthen the team spirit.

Collaborative code ownership

In collective code ownership, the entire team is responsible for the code. Everyone works together to produce a quality product. As it should always be in agile teams, all team members are equal.

Collaborative code ownership is perceived with both advantages and disadvantages.

Advantages:

Knowledge is shared

When only one person is responsible for certain modules or functions, a knowledge silo is created. This leads to critical knowledge being limited to a smaller group of people or, even worse, to one person. When the team is collectively responsible for code, everyone learns. When more people have the knowledge to make a difference, product quality is bound to improve.

Better code

When many people contribute to the code, this leads to better overall code quality. Of course, this assumes that the people involved identify with their task, the improvement of the code, and the resulting product quality. With only one person coding in a module, the work performed is not constructively critiqued.

No dependence on one person

If only one person in a team knows a module or program, there is a significant dependency on that person, because if, for example, that person leaves the company, goes on vacation, or becomes ill, this can cause significant disruption. In an environment where the code is understood and maintained by several, this dependency and the associated risk is considerably less.

Higher quality through more self-correction

If only one person knows the code within a feature or module, code reviews become a farce. Apart from being able to make high-level abstract comments, no real improvements can be suggested. When multiple people are involved, code correction and review is automatic, and thus quality improvement is built into the development process.

Knowledge transfer

Most people stagnate in terms of their competence development when they perform the same work again. One of the ways this happens is when companies establish specific roles and responsibilities in the development team. It is continuous learning that enhances the developer's skills and keeps the mind active. Through constant interactions and discussions with better developers, one can learn a lot in a short period of time.

Support for the development of agile teams

Collective code ownership almost automatically leads to a self-organizing team.

According to Scrum, individual team members should select the work of their choice. It should never be assigned to a specific person or role beforehand.

Negative effects

Of course, this is also countered by possible negative effects:

- No one is accountable - if there is no appropriate motivation, collaborative code ownership can lead to a culture of "the other guy did it"

- Strongly dependent on the quality of the developers - Only a team of good developers will also benefit optimally from the approach. With poor or moderately good developers, code degradation can also occur.
- Generalization - The tendency to exchange that goes hand in hand with the approach can - at least in theory - also lead to high performers focusing too little on their special disciplines, which can result in a drop in quality within the team.

Quintessence

All in all, collaborative code ownership is certainly not a panacea - but it can make a significant contribution to improving product quality if used correctly and responsibly.

Freeze - validate results and establish continuous improvement

If we move in an agile context, we must be aware that this means - if the initiative is to be successful - a long-term, actually even unlimited commitment to continuous improvement of the chosen approach. Although there are many different approaches and concepts for continuous improvement, "Kaizen" is often presented as the approach in this context. However, it also seems legitimate to use other approaches and concepts, as long as they serve the purpose of identifying experience gained and using it as a basis for tackling and implementing improvements.

Continuous improvement and Kaizen

When we talk about continuous improvement - whether this happens within the framework of the three pillars of Scrum (Transparency - Review - Adaptation) or the DMAIC circle (Define, Measure, Analyze, Improve and Control) - it is always about the three basic steps: first noticing and prioritizing things, taking action and sharing the lessons learned to ensure that experiences do not have to be made all over again by everyone.

A central aspect for continuous improvement is a team that identifies with the organization and wants to be successful. In this context, the research of Douglas MacGregor should be mentioned.

He defined "Theory X" and "Theory Y", which he used to describe different employee images.

Theory X states: *"Man has an innate aversion to work and tries to avoid it wherever possible. Due to his reluctance to work, he usually has to be forced, directed, guided and threatened with punishment in order to make a productive contribution to the achievement of organizational goals. He wants to be "taken by the hand" because he has too little ambition, prefers routine tasks, and seeks security. He shies away from any responsibility. Therefore, the manager must specify every step of action in detail, vigorously instruct and lead, and strictly control. Only in this way is efficient work execution possible. Remuneration alone cannot make people try hard enough. This means that external controls and punishments, as well as coercion, are needed when rules are violated. His behavior is governed by the majority opinion.*

The assumptions of Theory X are essentially the same as the assumptions of Taylorism. [6]*"*

Theory Y states: *"For humans, work has a high value and is an important source of satisfaction, because they are naturally willing to perform and are motivated from within. The most important work incentives are the satisfaction of ego needs and the pursuit of self-actualization. Therefore, conditions must be created that motivate people, for example through more self-determination, greater areas of responsibility, more flexible organizational structures, group and project work, etc. If the person identifies with the goals of the organization, then external controls are not necessary. This is because he will take responsibility and develop his own initiative. Creativity is also encouraged and demanded. Since this individual is committed to the goals of his organization, he will act in favor of the organizational goals. The individual possesses a high degree of imagination, judgment, and ingenuity to solve organizational problems.*

The assumptions of Theory Y essentially correspond to assumptions of the human relations concept. Theory Y is consistent with most corporate mission statements."

It is important to understand that there is no such thing as "Theory X" employees and "Theory Y" employees, but that employees can be either one or the other based on the conditions they find and experience. A leader who sees his or her employees as "Theory X" employees and guides them through close management, control and appropriate sanctioning will perceive his or her assumption to be just as correct as a leader who perceives his or her employees as motivated and proactive and sees himself or herself as a "servant leader" in the role of providing his or her team with the appropriate framework conditions so that they can work accordingly.

Employees who are managed according to Theory X will be reluctant to take initiatives because any change is perceived by them fundamentally as a risk of expected sanctions. Employees in the context of Theory Y, on the other hand, will approach approaches to continuous improvement - with the risk that errors may arise in the process - as normal measures.

"Freeze" as a keyword initially gives the impression that it is about us reaching a certain status or maturity, as it were, which is then virtually fixed and not changed further. Nothing could be further from agile thinking. Rather, freezing involves not only capturing a state, but also implementing a mindset and corresponding processes for continuous review and improvement. This, however, requires active and motivated cooperation of the team(s), which can only be achieved by teams that function and are managed according to Theory Y.

Turning "Theory X" teams into "Theory Y" teams requires a relatively large amount of effort, because this necessarily requires a corresponding mindset in an organization and especially among the leaders. Only if the framework conditions are created, a change in the team itself will be possible and even there only through supportive coaching and support.

---

[1] Leading Change, John Kotter
[2] https://www.ncbi.nlm.nih.gov/pmc/articles/PMC1765804/pdf/v013p0ii22.pdf

[3] http://web.mit.edu/curhan/www/docs/Articles/15341_Readings/Group_Dynamics/Tuckman_1965_Developmental_sequence_in_small_groups.pdf
and
http://faculty.wiu.edu/P-Schlag/articles/Stages_of_Small_Group_Development.pdf

[4] Hackman JR. The psychology of self-management in organizations. In: Pallack MS, Perloff RO Psychology and work: Productivity, change, and employment. Washington, DC: American Psychological Association ; 1986.

[5] Wikipedia.com - Accessed 12-2020

[6] Source of both quotes: https://de.wikipedia.org/wiki/X-Y-Theorie

Afterword

Leadership is an increasingly important topic in many organizations. Conventional approaches to leadership date back to a time when we were operating in a complicated environment in which organizations were faced with complicated but causally comprehensible frameworks. The concept for mastering such a world was simple: someone had to have a clear plan (leadership) and ensure that this plan was defined so simply and clearly that it could be understood by every employee. Once that was in place, the foundation for successful business existed. Many of our leaders did their training in this context.

Today, we find ourselves in a different situation in most environments. In many industries and contexts, the world has not become more complicated, but more complex. Many processes can no longer be represented so simply in causal impact chains. We are in a VUCA world in which the number of influencing variables is too diverse, changes are too rapid, and we no longer rely on maximum individual performance by employees, but only the interaction, synergy, experience, and knowledge of employees produce the necessary results that enable an organization to deal with everyday challenges.

If we want to perceive leadership correctly in this context, it is also necessary to question and, if necessary, adjust our own leadership and attitude to leadership.

This book is intended to provide suggestions for a leader in the context of DevOps and to provide clues as to which technical or methodological areas or which mindset lend themselves to further deepening.

Literature List

Bonaparte, Tony H. *Peter Drucker: Contributions to Business Enterprise.* New York University Press, 1970.

Burns, James McGregor. *Leadership.* Perennial, 1979.

Carr, Nicholas G. *Does IT Matter: Information Technology and the Corrosion of Competitive Advantage.* Harvard Business School Press, 2010.

Collins, James Charles. *Level 5 Leadership: the Triumph of Humility and Fierce Resolve.* Harvard Business Review, 2001.

Fröschle Hans-Peter. *DevOps.* Springer Vieweg, 2017.

Halstenberg Jürgen, et al. *DevOps Ein Uberblick.* Springer Fachmedien Wiesbaden GmbH, 2020.

Kotter, John P. *Leading Change.* Harvard Business Review Press, 2012.

Kotter, John P., and Rebecca Solow. *Our Iceberg Is Melting: Changing and Succeeding under Any Conditions.* Macmillan, 2017.

Leffingwell, Dean. *Scaled Agile Framework Reference Guide.* Addison-Wesley, 2016.

MULLER, PAUL C. *AGILE LEADERSHIP IM SCRUM-KONTEXT: Servant Leadership Fur Agile Leader Und Solche, Die Es... Werden Wollen.* BOOKS ON DEMAND, 2020.

Meister, Curt W. *DevOps - Erfolgreich Entwicklung Und IT-Betrieb Verbinden Grundlagen Und Werkzeuge für Eine Erfolgreiche DevOps-Implementierung.* BoD - Books on Demand, 2020.

Sward, David S. *Measuring the Business Value of Information Technology: Practical Strategies for IT and Business Managers.* Intel Press, 2006.

www.ingramcontent.com/pod-product-compliance
Lightning Source LLC
Chambersburg PA
CBHW020709180526
45163CB00008B/3003